Minimalist Living Explained

Why Less is More!

By: Asher Wright

Publishers Notes

Disclaimer

This publication is intended to provide helpful and informative material. It is not intended to diagnose, treat, cure, or prevent any health problem or condition, nor is intended to replace the advice of a physician. No action should be taken solely on the contents of this book. Always consult your physician or qualified health-care professional on any matters regarding your health and before adopting any suggestions in this book or drawing inferences from it.

The author and publisher specifically disclaim all responsibility for any liability, loss or risk, personal or otherwise, which is incurred as a consequence, directly or indirectly, from the use or application of any contents of this book.

Any and all product names referenced within this book are the trademarks of their respective owners. None of these owners have sponsored, authorized, endorsed, or approved this book.

Always read all information provided by the manufacturers' product labels before using their products. The author and publisher are not responsible for claims made by manufacturers.

Paperback Edition

Manufactured in the United States of America

DEDICATION

I dedicate this text to my parents. Without them I would never ever have the courage to try new things and to stand up for what I believe in no matter what.

TABLE OF CONTENTS

Publishers Notes 2

Dedication 3

Chapter 1- Minimalism- What Does It Mean? 5

Chapter 2- The Benefits Of Being A Minimalist 9

Chapter 3- Becoming A Minimalist 13

Chapter 4- Minimalism- Making Your Home Clutter-Free 17

Chapter 5- Shopping As A Minimalist 20

Chapter 6- Preparing A Budget And Handling Your Finances .. 24

Chapter 7- Minimalism- Frequently Asked Questions 28

About The Author 32

Chapter 1 - Minimalism - What Does It Mean?

We live in a vein world where we all strive to be the best and have the most. Eventually we come to a point in our lives where we realize that having more stuff does not equate to more happiness. When we reach this point we start seeing the desire in minimalism. Don't wait to reach this point, start minimizing now and see how your quality of life does not decrees with each thing you realize you don't need, but rather increases.

Dating Back To The Dawn Of Time

There is a modern trend towards voluntary simplicity, but this is not a new trend, rather it is just a rebirthed trend. The idea of not living with more than you need dates back for centuries from Leonardo Da Vinci, to Muhammad, to Confucius and even to Buddha. So now that we know who has practiced minimalism, it is time to have an understanding of what it is.

It is actually quite simple. Minimalism is not living with or without certain things, or even under a certain number of things. It does not mean you don't enjoy the finer things in life or that you become an environmentalist, if you aren't one already. Minimalism is highly individualized and will mean something different to everyone. But the one thing it has in common with everything is that it embraces the rule of not having what you don't need.

This does not mean you don't buy what you want, it means you want what you have. We have this tendency to want to fill spaces with "stuff." If we have an empty shelf in our kitchen, we have a desire to fill it, even if we have nothing to put on it. So we go out and buy stuff we don't need and didn't even want just so the space is not bare. By doing that we just spent money we didn't need to spend and got "stuff" that we wouldn't even notice is missing aside from the fact that there is once again a bare shelf.

<u>Have Less To Do And You Will Get More Done</u>

A huge benefit that all minimalists have experienced is being more productive. The truth is that the minimalist is not really more productive, but only appears to be since they have less to do. If you do spring cleaning by pulling everything out of your linen closet and washing it, you will find yourself doing loads of laundry for hours. The minimalist doesn't have this same problem because they only have the linens they use, they wash them as they become soiled, and they don't buy new ones until it becomes necessary. The minimalist now has less cleaning to do than their neighbor, and more importantly more time to enjoy life and its simple pleasures.

Happiness is not found in seeking more but rather in enjoying less, and the key to happiness is not in getting what you want but rather wanting what you have. If those lines sound familiar it is likely because they are age old sayings that have withstood the test of time for a simple reason, the fact that they are true. You can never keep up with your neighbor, someone will always have more than you, but what you will find when you are a minimalist is that all of the sudden you are the one with more.

A Tool That Should Be In Your Toolbox

If you have a hard time thinking of minimalism as more than just a trend for the hippies you are looking at it wrong. Minimalism is a way of life for some, but it is simply a tool for others. Have you ever had a cable bill that you have been paying for so long that one day you realize you lost hundreds of dollars on channels you don't even watch because you had to have the biggest and best package? Minimalism can be the tool to help you avoid that loss in the first place. Rather than wanting the biggest, you actually take the time to buy what you would use instead.

Another common place all of us could use minimalism is in shopping for groceries. How many times have you purchased more than you will eat because it is a better deal? We have all done this, but the minimalist uses the tool to actually determine if it is a good deal. If one pound of fruit is $5.00 but two pounds is $8.00 we always want to buy two pounds because is a better overall deal. Often we buy two pounds just to discover we can only eat one. Now a pound of fruit has gone to waist and $3.00 has gone down the drain. Sure the deal was good but the minimalist is now in a better position because he saved both money and food. Alternatively, if you can't pass up that deal, a minimalist will learn how to use it by freezing it, giving it away, cooking with it, or by some other means.

The less stuff one owns the less one's stuff owns him/her. Basically in short, a minimalist is a person who does more with less, lives life

Minimalist Living Explained

without being materialistic, but still has everything he wants to enjoy life. It is not as complicated as some make it out to be. Don't take my word for it though, try it for yourself, give it a few weeks, pack up your stuff and see if you can live without it. You won't regret the new freedom you will find and the control you will finally have on your own life.

Chapter 2 - The Benefits Of Being A Minimalist

Beyond its traditional sense, modern-day minimalism is more than just responsibilities and possessions. Minimalism can now be interpreted and considered to be a backlash against ownership and consumerism driving a contemporary society. Minimalist philosophy proponents even claim the increased quality of their lives with less sickness, stress and general fatigue. They contend that a minimalist lifestyle gets rid of everything that is inessential to a happy and healthy life. It is actually more on streamlining life for a stress-free one without complications as well as worries on any material possessions. Among its advantages are as follows:

Improvement In Financial Matters

Living a minimalist lifestyle usually encourages people to make necessary changes. This kind of life requires living material things in turn of a simple life and saving money. This may be in terms of vehicle gas and insurance elimination to save significant amount of money to pay for its repair, maintenance alongside things like phone and cable bills.

Find The Work That You Are Passionate About

Minimalism allows you to find the right job not for the paycheck, but for passion. It provides you a positive difference in choosing a job that definitely adds value to everyone other than yourself. This job that you really love to do ever since, one that exactly fits your personality and one that challenges you to aim for personal growth. As a result, you'll be able to enjoy working with your co-employees and you will feel valued, trusted and appreciated. It makes the values of your preferred company in alignment with your own values. This also leads to a result-oriented and flexible culture that values family brings life balance and satisfaction.

Opportunity For Rest

As always said and as many experts claim, there really is a serious danger when one loses the natural rhythm between work and rest. It is dangerous for the emotional well-being, relationships, physical body and spirituality. However, through minimalism, we can always guard the natural rhythm of life as it offers great opportunity for rest, enjoyment and refreshment.

Stress Reduction

In today's society, stress has been an issue for many adults in terms of things they want or need, bill payment, car maintenance, schedule or daily routine, keep up clutter and money. All these factors of stress can now be decreased or eliminated when you choose to live a minimalist way of life. This will eradicate all your worries that make you stressed out. Just imagine a minimalist home with less or no clutter and a calming environment.

Attaining The Freedom You Deserve

One feels freedom when everything around him is just new, organized and simple. This will be a lot different with a work desk, for instance, that has three bookcases, stacks of cluttered paper and other distractions that may lead to a stressful work environment. At home, one can make a last-minute decision when having short or long travel as well as easy movement from one place to another. The sense of freedom from minimalism is definitely refreshing. It can even define one's life it is more than just a mere feeling.

Asher Wright
Finding Things A Lot Easier

Usually, people tend to panic when they fail to find something they badly need at a minimal time. When you're living a minimalist lifestyle, you tend to organize things in a way that you will have easy access to them. This will then help you find what you are looking for.

Having Quality Time For Loved Ones And Interests

One of the promises of minimalism is to have quality time spent with friends, family and interests. You will have fewer things to cleanup and maintain when your stuff is less, giving you enough time for the most valuable things in life. A minimalist lifestyle can even afford you additional time to seek for your passions and become more focused and relaxed.

Having Good Insight Towards The Environment

The environment started out with perfection; that should be honored by taking good care of it. Less consumption of the environment results in less negative impact on it and great benefit to everyone. You are actually giving Earth a great help should you prefer not to use extra appliances requiring more kilowatts. It also makes a big difference if you're living a minimalist lifestyle of not using any vehicle that produces pollution and smog.

A More Concentrated Heart

Minimalism encourages a way of life that invests less on material possessions as the heart goes to the most important things in life. The heart seems to concentrate on valuable investments in social causes, child rearing and relationships, as these are the places where life's investment goes.

Minimalist Living Explained
<u>Additional Room Of Margin</u>

Having additional room that is related to physical attributes reflects a minimalist lifestyle. Just think of a very busy schedule without room for recreation, which does not open you to new opportunities for something that is either new or better. Remember that a pre-occupied schedule leaves no room for any addition. It is also a good reason to do things that can be counter-productive.

<u>Displaying The Most Valuable Things In Life</u>

There has been a misconception on how people view the minimalistic lifestyle as a way of removing all material possessions from one's life. The truth to the matter is that it is all about making the most significant decision in life and getting rid of any distraction.

With these benefits that minimalism offer to everyone, one can surely say that being simple and happy after all is readily achievable.

CHAPTER 3- BECOMING A MINIMALIST

Becoming a minimalist can be a major change for anyone. As mentioned in chapter 1, becoming a minimalist requires you to basically reduce the amount of belongs that you have and improve the way that you use your time. Minimalists will not buy anything that they really do not need to have. In addition a minimalist also learns how to do things in less time than what other people use.

If becoming a minimalist is something that is being considered it should be important to remember that the change cannot happen overnight. And that taking little steps will make the process so much easier. Becoming a minimalist isn't just about removing items; it is about time management as well. If you are interested in

Minimalist Living Explained

becoming a minimalist, hopefully, with any luck the suggestions below will be of some help.

One of the ways to become a minimalist is to not only remove one unnecessary item, but to completely get rid of the one item. Selecting this item in the beginning should not be that difficult, walk around your home or storage area, select one thing and remove it. This item can be donated, thrown away or sold, it just has to go. Try removing one unnecessary item per day.

Another starting block is to find an area in the home or storage area that is just basically cluttered up with things that have not been used for a while. These things are always put away with good intentions of using them at some point in the future. They may have been put in this place years ago. Many times when people start to look into these storage areas they are even surprised that they still have some of these things. This means that they already thought they had gotten rid of it, so they might as well remove it and move on.

Choose one spot, measure it off if you want, put some type of barrier around it if needed. This spot is to be an item free zone. As time progress and it becomes easier to remove more than one item at a time it is not uncommon to say, I may want this later, and then put it someplace else. This is how things become saved and forgotten. This one spot should be considered a safe zone and nothing should be placed inside of it. Over time this safe zone space will grow.

There is a difference between shopping and buying. Shopping is when people will walk around a store looking at things that they may or may not need, but there is a want. Buying is when people go into a store with a well written list; they go in get the items on the list and get out. When trying to become a minimalist becoming a buyer instead of a shopper is a good move. Write a list of things that are needed, and then review the list to make sure that the items are really needed. There is a good chance that at least one of the items isn't really needed at all.

We as people like to have clothes, often we have things that we have not worn in almost a year. And many have clothes that no longer fit, or aren't in style. Removing these articles of clothing will help to bring order to a closet or dresser in addition to removing more things that are not really needed. Chapter 5 will provide additional tips on how to make wise decisions when purchasing food, clothing and other items.

Some of the ways to become a minimalist is to change on the inside, it really isn't just about removing physical items, it is also about a change in the way we think. Our personal actions and decisions affect minimalism as much as any item does. Below are some suggestions about saving time on some things so that the time can be applied to doing other things.

One thing that almost everyone is guilty of is checking emails repeatedly and surfing the social media circuit. Many people have to work with a computer; many spend most of their day using a computer for work. However, how many times does that email really need to be checked? How many times had the email been checked when there was actually some task that could have been done during that same time? Forms of social media can also be a deterrent to getting things done. Just these couple of things mentioned can make a task take longer just by them taking away from the actual task.

Procrastination is another big problem that many people should try to work on when it comes to saving time. The old saying about putting off tomorrow what can be done today has never been so

Minimalist Living Explained

true. The things that we continually put off will always come back around and usually the result is that we look like we are unorganized and in other cases it looks very unprofessional.

Trying to become a minimalist in part is removing the things that can be distracting. This does not mean that in order to be a minimalist a person has to be about all work and no play. It is almost the complete opposite; there is a large part of the time saved from living this way that will allow plenty of free time. After the ways of a minimalist have been learned and applied to everyday life, there will almost seem to be a freedom that many people have not felt in a long time, if they have ever felt it at all.

Chapter 4- Minimalism- Making Your Home Clutter-Free

The minimalist lifestyle is one that is so different from others. As noted in previous chapters, people that are minimalists live on the philosophy to own only what they need. This means they get rid of things that they really do not need to have. This means cutting expenses in order to save money. As a result, people who live this way may end up with cluttered homes. Other minimalists have the exact opposite problem. They get rid of everything and end up having hardly anything.

If a minimalist has a cluttered home, it is probably because this person views everything with value. This type of person accepts anything that is free. He or she may stop and look through trash just to find things that have value. This person will not spend money on things he or she does not need, but it may be hard to say no to things that do not cost any money – even if these are things the person does not really need. The end result of this can be a cluttered home. Living in a cluttered home is not a good thing, for many reasons, but there are ways to change this.

The first step is to make a plan. The best type of plan is one that involves a room-by-room cleaning. A deep cleaning would be perfect for clearing out a cluttered home. Make a list of rooms in your home and choose one room to start in. Starting in a lightly-cluttered room might be the best idea. This is a good idea because this room would not need a lot of work. Once you are finished cleaning it, you may feel good about the way it looks. This may give you the motivation you need to keep going through all of the other rooms in your home.

Minimalist Living Explained

As you clean this first room, make several piles. As a minimalist you might have trouble throwing things away that you could use, but you are going to have to part with some things. Make one pile for things to throw away, and make another pile for things you can sell at a garage sale. If you can sell some of the things you own, you will make money. This is beneficial for living this type of lifestyle, and this may give you an incentive to put things in this pile. When you have gone through everything, clear out your piles. Throw the garbage away, and carry the garage sale items to your garage.

The final step for this room is to clean it. Dust the furniture, scrub or vacuum the floor. Shine the room up so that it looks great. Once you see the room in this condition, you will want the rest of your home to look like this. To do this, you can continue by starting with the next room on your list. As you do this, your home will slowly change from a cluttered mess to a place that is neat, clean, and shiny. One of the best parts is that you can make some money by doing this. When you have your garage sale, you will have the perfect opportunity to generate some cash.

Now that the house is perfectly clean, you will have to come up with ways to keep it this way. If you tend to be a junk collector, you will still have these tendencies. If you continue living the way you used to, your house will eventually end up full of clutter again. One good rule of thumb is to think before you bring anything in your home. Think about whether it is something you really need or not. If it is something you could live without, do not bring it inside – even if the item is free. It will take intention to live in a clutter-free home, and you will have to think before you carry anything in with you.

The next step is coming up with a cleaning schedule. Even if you stop bringing clutter in your home, your home can still end up cluttered, messy, and dirty. Write out a weekly schedule to help you with this. A good idea is to choose a different room to clean each day. You could make Mondays your day to clean the kitchen. Tuesdays could be for the bathrooms, and so on. A schedule like this forces you to clean every room on a regular basis, and this will keep your house clutter-free.

Another idea is to have a garage sale each year. Not only will this add money to your budget, but it will help you keep junk out of your house. As you begin to live a clutter-free life, you may begin to really enjoy it. You may feel happier in life. You may be more content with the things you have. You may really love the way you live.

Living a life as a minimalist is not always an easy option to take, but it is very fulfilling. People that live like this can tell you how satisfying it is. They are able to focus on the more important things in life, and they are able to help others more. They have more time and money, and they are just happier in general. You can live like this too. It will take adjustments to your schedule, life, and habits. All of these changes will be positive and good for you and your family, and that is what is important.

Chapter 5 - Shopping As A Minimalist

Minimalist shopping requires a different focus than many people might think. Since minimalist thinking involves reducing or preventing the accumulation of possessions, shopping takes on a different meaning for those people attempting to live this way. To be clear though, there are some things that even minimalist purchase such as groceries while there are other things which won't even cross some minimalists' minds to buy like a car or a house. Here are some tips to shop like a minimalist for both those common items and the big purchases.

For the common items like groceries, clothing, and similar merchandise, the primary concern is flexibility. Which purchases allow the minimalist the ability to use it in multiple ways? For example, an apple pie serves as a dessert and little else, whereas buying apples, sugar, and either dough or the ingredients for the dough allows the minimalist to transform the raw ingredients into a pie or any number of other recipes. For these reasons, here are some handy tips to remember with a brief explanation of why I recommend them.

Asher Wright
<u>In The Grocery Store</u>

Maximize your shopping around the outside of the store. The areas around the outside of most grocery stores contain the fruits and vegetables, the freezers where meat and seafood is stored, and other items which typically require refrigeration because there are few preservatives in them. These raw ingredients combine into endless recipes and can allow for proper nutrition as well as variety. Of course, the baked goods section falls into this area as well, so a little caution might be advised, but otherwise this rule of thumb works well.

<u>Shop In The Spice Aisle</u>

Going the minimalist route for groceries can lead to bland food without knowledge of how to add flavors and that means spices. Five or six spices increases flavor options immeasurably. Test out a new one each week until you find five or six which work well. For those you don't like, give them as gifts to friends who like to cook.

<u>Regarding Clothes</u>

Start with a classic look. Like the food, the goal of clothes purchases should focus on flexibility. Find a few classic looks which appeal to you and require few accessories and go from there. An example for men, the classic khaki and button up shirt, allows a man to own two or three pairs of pants and five or six shirts and still gives vast variety to their appearance each day. This look might be more formal than some people prefer, so find one that works.

Find durable apparel to double as interior or exterior clothes. Long-sleeve shirts can serve as a light jacket in the spring and on cool mornings. This reduces or eliminates the need to have a jacket. Make sure there is a solution for rainy days.

For larger purchases, the focus remains on flexibility, but also on how long the item will be needed. Consider these things when making larger purchases.

Consider The Cost Of Ownership

Perhaps the biggest consideration for the minimalist, the cost of ownership captures many elements. Some common questions to consider:

- What ongoing maintenance costs, both monetary and time, are required to keep this item in good working order?
- What space must be given up to keep and use this item? Will this result in additional costs in time and money?
- What must be sacrificed so that this item can be afforded both today and in the future?
- If there are additional monetary costs, how can these be covered and what will they cost in other time and sacrifice?

"Shopping" Doesn't Mean "Purchasing"

Consider renting the item for a certain amount of time. This can be done through outright rental or by purchasing an item with the knowledge that it will be resold later. For instance, someone planning to move could rent a truck which then gets returned after the move is completed or they could purchase a truck, move, and resell the truck a short time later. Both of the example options have various costs associated with them, but in either case, the minimalist completes the move without having the long-term costs of keeping up the truck needed for the move.

What Else Can It Do?

If purchasing the item is the best option, consider what other needs it can meet. Can friends and family benefit from your possessing it? Can it serve another purpose? For instance, a boat can move a person across water, friends and family can use the boat also, and it can also be used to store some items inside. Perhaps the storage space for the boat provides enough space for additional storage. In this example, remember that storage space is not a great benefit for most minimalists. However, the minimalist who likes boats might actually decide to purchase a boat to live on and eliminate the costs of home ownership or the headaches of renting living space.

Look For Durability

If this product is worth owning why not purchase the model which is most likely to last the longest? Every additional year the product survives and remains useful is another year when additional purchasing decisions are not required. Plus, the better condition of the product should make selling, trading, or giving it away a better option, should the need arise.

Remember, minimalist doesn't mean having nothing or having inferior items. Minimalists can have nice things; they choose to have fewer things.

Chapter 6- Preparing A Budget And Handling Your Finances

Living life as a minimalist is certainly not the most popular approach you will see in today's culture. So many people spend more than they earn, and they own way more than they need. Living as a minimalist means having only the things you need. Because of this, preparing a budget and handling finances in this manner is quite easy. Not only is it easy, but it is actually the most important and necessary thing you can do.

Most people do not start out living as minimalists. If you do that is great, but it is not common. In other words, most people have to transition into this lifestyle. This may not be an easy transition, but it will help you improve so many different aspects of your life.

Creating a budget and learning how to handle your finances will take some time, but there are easy ways to do this. The first step is to write down your monthly expenses and any debts you owe. Make two separate lists of these things. The first list should include every normal expense you have monthly. This includes rent, mortgage payments, car payments, utilities, credit card bills, and any other regular expenses you have each month. The second list should include all of the debts you have. Include your house, car, credit card bills, and anything else you owe a lump sum of money for.

Now comes the fun part. You need to look at your list of debts to see if there is anything you can eliminate. If you have a house, do you think you should sell it? It would free up money each month, and it would get rid of a large chunk of debt. If you have a car with a large loan, maybe you could sell it and buy a car that does not have a loan. Cutting out large debts is vital if you want to live as a minimalist. You will be surprised to find out how much money this can help you save each month and year.

The next step is to look at the list of monthly expenses. As you scan this list, place a checkmark by the expenses that you cannot get rid of. This includes utility bills and insurance expenses. Mark anything that is a necessity, but keep in mind what a necessity really is. After you are finished doing this, look at each of the expenses that you did not mark. Go through each one and ask yourself if you really need it. For example, look at your cellphone bill. Yes, most people have cell phones, but is owning a cellphone something that you could not live without? The truth is that you could live without it. It might take some readjustments to your life, but you could do without it.

Another good item to look at is cable TV. Most homes have multiple TVs, and most of these TVs are attached to a satellite dish or cable. The money you spend on this can add up to a significant amount each year, and this is one bill you could also do away with. Little by little, you will have to get rid of luxury expenses. One of the key features of living as a minimalist is that you will not own things you do not really need. By living this way, you can cut your expenses down by hundreds of dollars each month. While this thought might scare you, it is important to realize that luxury items do not bring happiness. People who live as minimalists are often happier, more content with life, and are able to discover their purposes in life.

Once you have eliminated all you can, you can sit down with your new budget. Compare the amount of income you have each month to your new monthly expense amount. For the first time, you might actually have a disposable income. Disposable income is the difference between how much you make and how much your expenses are. This money can be used however you choose.

As a minimalist, you should look at this amount and determine what to do with it. You will need to budget out a certain amount for groceries, gas, and other normal expenditures, but you will still have money left. The best thing to do is come up with a savings plan. Make saving money a normal monthly expense. By doing this, you will actually save a lot of money. You might want to create your own investment and savings plan, or you might want to hire an investment advisor for help. You can choose either method, but this is a very important step in creating a budget. Your budget will guide your purchases and expenditures, and it is necessary for this lifestyle.

Learning how to live without things you do not need will require a period of adjustment, but as you learnt in Chapter 2, there are so many benefits of this. You may find that the quality of your life improves from this. Your attitude towards life and others may also improve. You will have financial freedom, money in the bank, and so much more. You will not have to spend all your time working extra jobs just to pay for things you really do not need. The minimalist lifestyle is certainly not the most popular way to live today, but it is a choice that offers true happiness, contentment, and joy in your life.

Chapter 7- Minimalism- Frequently Asked Questions

Many people have heard the term "Minimalism", yet the majority of those same people are likely to have a host of unanswered questions surrounding the true meaning of the term. While there is no set definition for the term, there are quite a few questions that can assist in bringing clarity to those seeking a deeper understanding of how a minimalist lives. Although there are no hard and fast answers, people interested in minimalism may seek answers to the following types of questions:

Why Would Someone Choose A Minimalistic Lifestyle?

As stated in other chapters, the most common reason is to simply have more time and energy to engage in the activities that each person actually prefers to do, as opposed to that which they feel required to do. If, for example, your household bills include multiple car payments, televisions, phones, electronic devices, expensive prepackaged food, etc., a high paying job will be required to cover those expenses. On the other hand, if someone chooses to live in a smaller home with minimal electronics, prepares their own food, and normally rides a bicycle as opposed to using a car, they will have far less to cover in expenses, leaving more time available for what they truly love to do.

Can I Own A Car If I Am A Minimalist?

Everything is relative. If you are a mother of 4 children who lives on a farm, hosts a homeschooling group several times a week, and chooses to own a vehicle to run errands in town occasionally, most people could easily classify you as a minimalist. If, on the other hand, you live alone in an urban area with easily accessible public transportation, justifying the ownership of a car in the name of minimalism would be very challenging.

Can A Minimalist Watch Television?

Truthfully most probably do not. However, that being said, there are always exceptions. Most minimalists choose not to watch television as a result of choosing to prioritize their time in other activities which are generally more interactive and engaging than the passive act of watching television. One possible reason a minimalist family might use a television would be to offer homeschooled children a truly versatile educational tool, as the availability of high quality material for homeschooling curriculum on television is readily available when carefully selected. The main key is that most minimalists would not simply be "passing time" by watching "the tube"; it would be a much more conscious choice to do so.

Minimalist Living Explained

Is There A Certain Number Of Objects A Minimalist Can Own?

This is a question that reflects the value system of most minimalists. The idea behind minimalism is not necessarily to eliminate all of your stuff, but rather, to really make conscious choices about what we do choose to own and how we chose to use our time. For many minimalists, when they've made the choice to simplify their life, they simply find that they don't need very many material objects anymore. As a simple example, if a man decides he is going to grow a beard so that he no longer needs to be concerned about daily shaving, which eliminates the need to purchase razor blades. The same concept applies to everything; when you choose to simplify your life, you will simply need less material stuff. So while there is no set limit to how many objects someone living a minimalistic lifestyle can own, each object that they do choose to keep should really increase the overall quality of their life.

Can A Minimalist Have A Job?

Since it is nearly impossible to live without at least a small income in today's world, the reality is that many minimalists do still keep a job, although many choose to run a small business from home that allows them to earn the minimum amount of money they truly need to provide themselves with basic necessities. Since many minimalists also may raise a portion of their own food and provide many of their general needs more directly, their costs of living are likely to be substantially less than others. This can allow them the opportunity to develop a home craft or custom service they can provide and permits them to work a small number of hours per week to make ends meet financially.

Are Minimalists Poorly Educated?

The opposite is more commonly the case. Many minimalists have chosen to alter their lifestyle after spending a period of their life living conventionally. Some have left high paying careers and are highly educated. Minimalism is a conscious choice that people make after finding that their previous choices have not brought them fulfillment and happiness. It is well known that a common complaint of people in high paying and stressful jobs generally have low levels of overall satisfaction in life; it is those same people who are the most likely to turn to a life of minimalism after growing disconcerted with the system they formerly participated within.

<u>*Does Minimalism Mean A Person Lives In Poverty?*</u>

Definitely not, at least based on the opinions and happiness levels of those who choose this type of lifestyle. People who live in impoverished conditions generally feel that much is lacking in their lives; they may be seeking to improve their living conditions and always feel stuck with their current situation. People who consciously choose to live a minimalistic life are likely to have reduced the number of material objects they own, yet feel gratitude for that reduction, as it allows them more time to enjoy their life. There is no sense of lack, as the choice to have less material goods is a conscious one.

The list of questions that could be asked about minimalism is truly endless. The basic idea behind this lifestyle choice is that when you value your time more than your material goods, you will find you need far fewer material objects. While certainly not for everyone, those who have chosen to live a minimalistic lifestyle often find a path that leads them to more happiness than they had ever before experienced.

About The Author

Asher Wright learned certain things from his parents at an early age. Initially he was taught that it was not prudent to buy more than was needed nor was it prudent to spend more than what one had simply to keep up appearances. They were not minimalist but they were careful with what they spend and they did not attract debt. They saved and bought what they wanted.

As an adult Asher remembered these life lessons and applied them to everything that he did. When he was introduced to the concept of minimalism he was even more intrigued. He marveled at those individuals who could live with just the bare necessities.

www.ingramcontent.com/pod-product-compliance
Ingram Content Group UK Ltd.
Pitfield, Milton Keynes, MK11 3LW, UK
UKHW022217230426
12048UKWH00016BA/911